S0-ARM-704

Grade 1

Phonics

Vowels • Consonants
Letters & Sounds

A McGraw·Hill/Warner Bros. Workbook

Table of Contents

Table of Contents (continued)

Credits:
McGraw-Hill Learning Materials Editorial/Production Team
Vincent F. Douglas, B.S. and M. Ed.
Tracy R. Paulus
Jennifer P. Blashkiw

Design Studio
Mike Legendre; Creativity On Demand

Warner Bros. Worldwide Publishing Editorial/Production Team
Michael Harkavy   Charles Carney
Paula Allen   Allen Helbig
Victoria Selover   Sara Hunter

Illustrators
Cover and Interior: Animated Arts!™

McGraw-Hill
Consumer Products
A Division of The McGraw·Hill Companies

CONSONANTS: S

The sound at the beginning of **sun** is spelled by the letter **s**.

sun

Name the pictures. Circle each picture whose name begins with the sound of **s**.

CONSONANTS: M

The sound at the beginning of **mouse** is spelled by the letter **m**.

mouse

Name the pictures. Circle each picture whose name begins with the sound of **m**.

4

NAME _____

CONSONANTS: T

The sound at the beginning of **tent** is spelled by the letter **t**.

tent

Name the pictures. Circle each picture whose name begins with the sound of **t**.

NAME _____

REVIEW

Name the pictures. Write the letter that stands for the beginning sound of each picture name.

_____

_ _ _ _ _ _ _ _ _ _

_____

_____

_ _ _ _ _ _ _ _ _ _

_____

6
_____

_ _ _ _ _ _ _ _ _ _

_____

ENDING SOUNDS: S, M, T

The sound at the end of **bus** is spelled by the letter **s**.	bus
The sound at the end of **ham** is spelled by the letter **m**.	ham
The sound at the end of **cat** is spelled by the letter **t**.	cat

Name the pictures. Circle the letter that stands for the sound you hear at the end of each picture name.

s m ⓣ	s m t	s m t	s m t
s m t	s m t	s m t	s m t
s m t	s m t	s m t	s m t
s m t	s m t	s m t	s m t

7

CONSONANTS: P

The sound at the beginning of **pig** is spelled by the letter **p**.

pig

Name the pictures. Circle each picture whose name begins with the sound of **p**.

CONSONANTS: N

The sound at the beginning of **nest** is spelled by the letter **n.**

nest

Name the pictures. Circle each picture whose name begins with the sound of **n.**

CONSONANTS: C

The sound at the beginning of **car** is spelled by the letter **c**.

car

Name the pictures. Circle each picture whose name begins with the sound of **c**.

P, N, C

REVIEW

Name the pictures. Write the letter that stands for the beginning sound of each picture name.

n

11

ENDING SOUNDS:
P, N, C

The sound at the end of **moon** is spelled by the letter **n**.	moon
The sound at the end of **mop** is spelled by the letter **p**.	mop
The sound at the end of **magic** is spelled by the letter **c**.	magic

Name the pictures. Circle the letter that stands for the sound you hear at the end of each picture name.

(p) n c	p n c	p n c	p n c
p n c	p n c	p n c	p n c
p n c	p n c	p n c	p n c
p n c	p n c	p n c	p n c

12

CONSONANTS: K

The sound at the beginning of **kitten** is spelled by the letter **k**.

kitten

Name the pictures. Circle each picture whose name begins with the sound of **k**.

13

CONSONANTS: R

The sound at the beginning of **rose** is spelled by the letter **r**.

rose

Name the pictures. Circle each picture whose name begins with the sound of **r**.

CONSONANTS: B

The sound at the beginning of **ball** is spelled by the letter **b**.

ball

Name the pictures. Circle each picture whose name begins with the sound of **b**.

K,R, B

REVIEW

Name the pictures. Write the letter that stands for the beginning sound of each picture name.

k

NAME _____

ENDING SOUNDS: K, R, B

The sound at the end of **book** is spelled by the letter **k**. The sound at the end of **four** is spelled by the letter **r**. The sound at the end of **tub** is spelled by the letter **b**.	book four tub

Name the pictures. Circle the letter that stands for the sound you hear at the end of each picture name.

k r (b)	k r b	k r b	k r b
k r b	k r b	k r b	k r b
k r b	k r b	k r b	k r b
k r b	k r b	k r b	k r b

17

CONSONANTS:

The sound at the beginning of **jet** is spelled by the letter **j**.

jet

Name the pictures. Circle each picture whose name begins with the sound of **j**.

NAME

CONSONANTS: F

The sound at the beginning of **fish** is spelled by the letter **f**.

fish

Name the pictures. Circle each picture whose name begins with the sound of **f**.

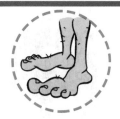

CONSONANTS: G

The sound at the beginning of **goat** is spelled by the letter **g**.

goat

Name the pictures. Circle each picture whose name begins with the sound of **g**.

NAME _____

J, F, G

REVIEW

Name the pictures. Write the letter that stands for the beginning sound of each picture name.

21

ENDING SOUNDS: F AND G

The sound at the end of **roof** is spelled by the letter **f**.	**roof**
The sound at the end of **bag** is spelled by the letter **g**.	**bag**

Name the pictures. Circle the letter that stands for the sound you hear at the end of each picture name.

	f (g)		f g		f g		f g
	f g		f g		f g		f g
	f g		f g		f g		f g
	f g		f g		f g		f g

22

CONSONANTS: H

The sound at the beginning of **horse** is spelled by the letter **h**.

horse

Name the pictures. Circle each picture whose name begins with the sound of **h**.

CONSONANTS: D

The sound at the beginning of **dog** is spelled by the letter **d**.

dog

Name the pictures. Circle each picture whose name begins with the sound of **d**.

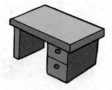 

CONSONANTS: Z

The sound at the beginning of **zoo** is spelled by the letter **z**.

ZOO

Name the pictures. Circle each picture whose name begins with the sound of **z**.

REVIEW

Name the pictures. Write the letter that stands for the beginning sound of each picture name.

h

26

NAME

CONSONANTS: W

The sound at the beginning of **watch** is spelled by the letter **w**.

watch

Name the pictures. Circle each picture whose name begins with the sound of **w**.

27

CONSONANTS: V

The sound at the beginning of **vase** is spelled by the letter **v**.

vase

Name the pictures. Circle each picture whose name begins with the sound of **v**.

CONSONANTS: L

The sound at the beginning of **lion** is spelled by the letter l.

lion

Name the pictures. Circle each picture whose name begins with the sound of l.

REVIEW

Name the pictures. Write the letter that stands for the beginning sound of each picture name.

_____   _____   _____

- - - - - - V - - - -   - - - - - - - - -   - - - - - - - - -

_____   _____   _____

_____   _____   _____

- - - - - - - - -   - - - - - - - - -   - - - - - - - - -

_____   _____   _____

_____   _____   _____

- - - - - - - - -   - - - - - - - - -   - - - - - - - - -

_____   _____   _____

ENDING SOUNDS: D AND L

The sound at the end of **road** is spelled by the letter **d**. The sound at the end of **girl** is spelled by the letter l.	road girl

Name the pictures. Circle the letter that stands for the sound you hear at the end of each picture name.

d (l)	d l	d l	d l
d l	d l	d l	d l
d l	d l	d l	d l
d l	d l	d l	d l

31

NAME _____

CONSONANTS: Y

The sound at the beginning of **yard** is spelled by the letter **y**.

yard

Name the pictures. Circle each picture whose name begins with the sound of **y**.

32

CONSONANTS: X

The sound at the end of **ax** is spelled by the letter **x**.

ax

Name the pictures. Circle each picture whose name ends with the sound of **x**.

  (additional pictures in rows)

33

CONSONANTS: Qu

The sound at the beginning of **quilt** is spelled by the letters **qu**.

quilt

Name the pictures. Circle each picture whose name begins with the sound of **qu**.

Y, QU

REVIEW

Name the pictures. Write the letter or pair of letters that stands for the beginning sound of each picture name.

_____

qu

35

REVIEW

Name the pictures. Write the letter that stands for the ending sound of each picture name.

_____

- - - - - m -

_____

_____

- -

_____

_____

- -

_____

PROGRESS CHECK

Name the pictures. Write the letters that stand for the beginning and ending sounds of each picture name.

d o   u   o

o   a   u

a   i   u

37

VOWELS: SHORT A

Fan has the short-**a** sound. This sound is usually spelled by the letter **a**.

fan

Name the pictures. Circle each picture whose name has the short-a sound.

VOWELS: SHORT I

Bib has the short-i sound. This sound is usually spelled by the letter i.

bib

Name the pictures. Circle each picture whose name has the short-i sound.

 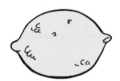 

39

REVIEW

Read the words and name the pictures. Circle the word that names each picture.

pin fan fin (pan)	hit mat mitt hat	lid lad lap lip
sit ax add six	bat bit miss mad	hit bag hat big
cat tap cap tip	pig dam dig pass	wag dig wig dad
mix fat map fit	rip sap sip ran	can zip cap big

40

VOWELS: SHORT O

Top has the short-o sound. This sound is usually spelled by the letter **o**.	top

Name the pictures. Circle each picture whose name has the short-o sound.

41

VOWELS: SHORT E

Bed has the short-**e** sound. This sound is usually spelled by the letter **e**.

bed

Name the pictures. Circle each picture whose name has the short-**e** sound.

NAME

REVIEW

SHORT O, E

Read the words and name the pictures. Circle the word that names each picture.

(box) fed bell fox	top ten men mop	jet pot job pet
hot men hen mop	doll pet well pot	egg ox fell fox
wet web cob cot	pop ten top pen	tell beg top bed
rod leg log red	fed hop hen mop	got net not get

43

VOWELS: SHORT U

Cup has the short-**u** sound. This sound is usually spelled by the letter **u**.

cup

Name the pictures. Circle each picture whose name has the short-**u** sound.

REVIEW

Read the words and name the pictures. Circle the word that names each picture.

(sun) suds sad cat	lid lad lip lap	mug mat man mud
cat cob cab cot	bag bed bad beg	pin pen peg pig
ran rug rag rub	bit beg bet bib	net nut men met
top tab tub tap	but bat bit bet	bug but bun bus

SHORT VOWELS

Name the pictures. Circle the letter that stands for the vowel sound in each picture name. Then write the letter to complete the picture name.

ⓐ e	i o	u e
b a t	p _ t	b _ d
a u	i a	o e
s _ n	p _ g	l _ g
a o	i e	o u
_ x	t _ n	b _ g

46

PROGRESS CHECK

Name the pictures. Write the letter to complete the picture name.

h a t   p _ t   w _ b

s _ n   s _ x   p _ g

b _ x   t _ g   h _ g

VOWELS: LONG A

Rake has the long-a sound. This sound is often spelled by **a** and silent **e**.

rake

Name the pictures. Circle each picture whose name has the long-a sound.

VOWELS: LONG I

Kite has the long-i sound. This sound is often spelled by **i** and silent **e**.

kite

Name the pictures. Circle each picture whose name has the long-i sound.

 9

  6

  5

49

REVIEW

Read the words and name the pictures. Circle the word that names each picture.

time tin tap (tape) 	kit can kite cane 	dim dime date dam 
pan van vine pine 	bit bike bite big 	ride rat ran rid 
hide hive hat hate 	miss mat mitt man 	dive dad did date 
lad lid like lake 	sat side safe sit 	pine pal pal pale 

50

NAME _____

VOWELS: LONG U

Tube has the long-u sound. This sound is often spelled by u and silent e.

tube

Name the pictures. Circle each picture whose name has the long-u sound.

51

REVIEW

LONG O, U

Read the words and name the pictures. Circle the word that names each picture.

cub cob cone (cube) 	rode ruler rod run 	top toss tube tub 
mop mug mole mule 	note nut not nose 	mule mug moss mole 
rule rose rod rug 	bone but bus box 	top tune tug tone 
rule run rope rot 	bone box bus bun 	note nut nose not 

REVIEW

LONG VOWELS

Name the pictures. Write the letters to complete the picture name.

h i v e   r _ p   t _ b

n _ t   m _ l   c _ b

b _ n   v _ n   l _ k

53

LONG VOWELS

Read each sentence and the words beside it. Circle, then write the word that makes sense in the sentence.

1. Nine bats are in the ___cave___ .

    (cave)
    came
    note

2. I may _____ a cape.

    vote
    make
    kite

3. What is his _____ ?

    name
    five
    nine

4. The lid is on the _____ .

    time
    tune
    tube

5. Did you _____ into the lake?

    dive
    hive
    live

6. Billy wants to _____ the bone.

    line
    hope
    hide

PROGRESS CHECK

Name the pictures. Write the letters to complete the picture name.

t u n e

n ___ n

k ___ t

l ___ k

t ___ p

r ___ p

v ___ n

m ___ l

r ___ b

VOWELS:
SHORT AND LONG

Name the pictures. Write the letter or letters to complete the picture name.

v i n e

r s

l k

w b

f v

f x

m l

b b

t n

PROGRESS CHECK

Name the pictures. Write the letter or letters to complete the picture name.

c _ v _

l _ k

p _ g

j _ t

r _ p

n _ n

t _ b

s _ n

f _ n

S BLENDS

In some words, the letter **s** comes before another consonant. To say these words, blend the sound of **s** with the sound of the consonant that follows it.

stop **skate**
smile **sleep**

Name the pictures. In each row, circle the picture or pictures that begin with the same sound as the first picture.

L BLENDS

In some words, the letter l follows another consonant. To say these words, blend the sound of the first consonant with the sound of l.

flower
play

Name the pictures. In each row, circle the picture or pictures that begin with the same sound as the first picture.

R BLENDS

In some words, the letter **r** follows another consonant. To say these words, blend the sound of the first consonant with the sound of **r**.

frog
brown
green

Name the pictures. In each row, circle the picture or pictures that begin with the same sound as the first picture.

 NAME

FINAL S BLENDS

At the end of some words, the letter **s** comes before another consonant. To say these words, blend the sound of **s** with the sound of that consonant.

a**sk**
ju**st**

Name the pictures. In each row, circle the picture or pictures that end with the same sound as the first picture.

PROGRESS CHECK

Read the words below. Then name the pictures. Write the word that names the picture.

drum	sled	desk	flag	snake
crab	nest	plate	frog	

  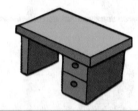

--- crab --- _____ _____

_____ _____ _____

_____ _____ _____

NAME

 REVIEW

Read the words and name the pictures. Circle the word that names each picture.

sail say (seal) see	pay pail peel peas 	bee beat beak beef 
tail team tea tray 	mail may meat meet 	ray rain read real 
play pay pain pail 	train tray rain tree 	hay heat heel hail 

63

PROGRESS CHECK

Read the words and name the pictures. Circle the word that names each picture.

(mail) mow 	snail snow 	try tray 
see seal 	bee by 	boat book 
soap seem 	bait boot 	hair hook 
bunny bean 	stay sky 	baby by 

ANSWER KEY

CONSONANTS: S

The sound at the beginning of **sun** is spelled by the letter **s**.

sun

Name the pictures. Circle each picture whose name begins with the sound of **s**.

saddle	saw	mailbox	seven
mouse	six	wolf	four
socks	sandwich	ham	soap
seal	key	squirrel	pumpkin

3

CONSONANTS: M

The sound at the beginning of **mouse** is spelled by the letter **m**.

mouse

Name the pictures. Circle each picture whose name begins with the sound of **m**.

money	monkey	moon	rake
mountain	tent	map	mitten
mop	fish	cannon	mirror
seven	magnet	match	milk

4

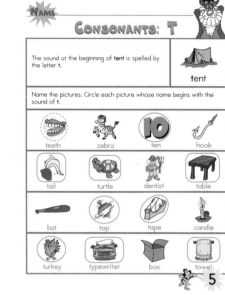

CONSONANTS: T

The sound at the beginning of **tent** is spelled by the letter **t**.

tent

Name the pictures. Circle each picture whose name begins with the sound of **t**.

teeth	zebra	ten	hook
tail	turtle	dentist	table
bat	top	tape	candle
turkey	typewriter	box	towel

5

REVIEW

Name the pictures. Write the letter that stands for the beginning sound of each picture name.

mice	saw	tent
m	s	t
sandwich	turtle	mirror
s	t	m
match	typewriter	six
m	t	s

6

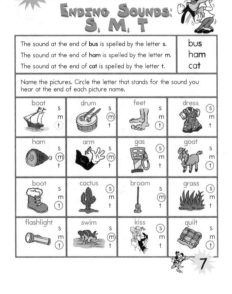

ENDING SOUNDS: S, M, T

The sound at the end of **bus** is spelled by the letter **s**.
The sound at the end of **ham** is spelled by the letter **m**.
The sound at the end of **cat** is spelled by the letter **t**.

bus
ham
cat

Name the pictures. Circle the letter that stands for the sound you hear at the end of each picture name.

boat s m (t)	drum s (m) t	feet s m (t)	dress (s) m t
ham s (m) t	arm s (m) t	gas (s) m t	goat s m (t)
boot s m (t)	cactus s (m) t	broom s (m) t	grass (s) m t
flashlight s m (t)	swim s (m) t	kiss (s) m t	quilt s m (t)

7

CONSONANTS: P

The sound at the beginning of **pig** is spelled by the letter **p**.

pig

Name the pictures. Circle each picture whose name begins with the sound of **p**.

puppy	pocket	pen	leaf
pitcher	tie	pineapple	pumpkin
mop	pot	pencil	ten
salad	peanuts	tent	piano

8

65

ANSWER KEY

Consonants: N

NAME

The sound at the beginning of **nest** is spelled by the letter n.

nest

Name the pictures. Circle each picture whose name begins with the sound of n.

net (circled)	nine	top	neck
nose	water tower	tape	nail
nuts	needle	raccoon	candle
tiger	nurse	butterfly	newspaper

9

Consonants: C

NAME

The sound at the beginning of **car** is spelled by the letter c.

car

Name the pictures. Circle each picture whose name begins with the sound of c.

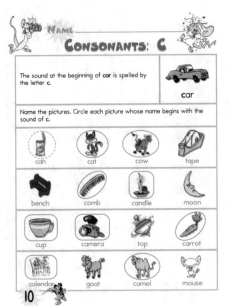

can (circled)	cat	cow	tape
bench	comb	candle	moon
cup	camera	top	carrot
calendar	goat	camel	mouse

10

Review

NAME

Name the pictures. Write the letter that stands for the beginning sound of each picture name.

nuts	canoe	pin
n	c	p
cactus	nine	pot
c	n	p
pedal	pen	net
p	p	n

11

Ending Sounds: P, N, C

NAME

The sound at the end of **moon** is spelled by the letter n. — moon

The sound at the end of **mop** is spelled by the letter p. — mop

The sound at the end of **magic** is spelled by the letter c. — magic

Name the pictures. Circle the letter that stands for the sound you hear at the end of each picture name.

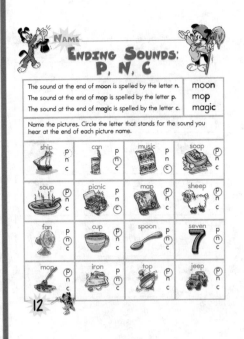

ship — p (n) c	can — (n) p c	music — p n (c)	soap — (p) n c
soup — (p) n c	picnic — p n (c)	map — (p) n c	sheep — (p) n c
fan — p (n) c	cup — (p) n c	spoon — p (n) c	seven — p (n) c
mop — (p) n c	iron — p (n) c	top — (p) n c	jeep — (p) n c

12

Consonants: K

NAME

The sound at the beginning of **kitten** is spelled by the letter k.

kitten

Name the pictures. Circle each picture whose name begins with the sound of k.

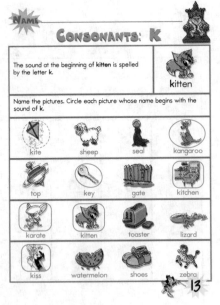

kite (circled)	sheep	seal	kangaroo
top	key	gate	kitchen
karate	kitten	toaster	lizard
kiss	watermelon	shoes	zebra

13

Consonants: R

NAME

The sound at the beginning of **rose** is spelled by the letter r.

rose

Name the pictures. Circle each picture whose name begins with the sound of r.

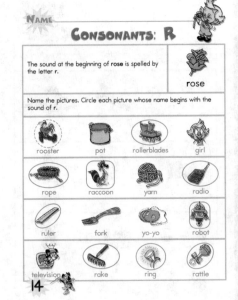

rooster (circled)	pot	rollerblades	girl
rope	raccoon	yarn	radio
ruler	fork	yo-yo	robot
television	rake	ring	rattle

14

66

ANSWER KEY

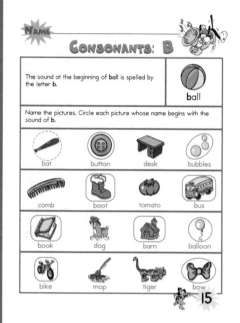

CONSONANTS: B

The sound at the beginning of **ball** is spelled by the letter **b**.

ball

Name the pictures. Circle each picture whose name begins with the sound of **b**.

bat	button	desk	bubbles
comb	boot	tomato	bus
book	dog	barn	balloon
bike	mop	tiger	bow

15

REVIEW

Name the pictures. Write the letter that stands for the beginning sound of each picture name.

kitten	radio	key
k	r	k
ruler	bottle	belt
r	b	b
raccoon	ring	kangaroo
r	r	k

16

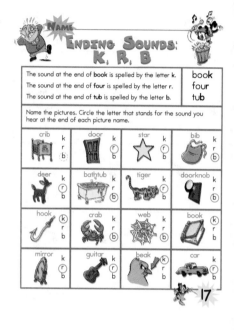

ENDING SOUNDS: K, R, B

The sound at the end of **book** is spelled by the letter **k**.
The sound at the end of **four** is spelled by the letter **r**.
The sound at the end of **tub** is spelled by the letter **b**.

book
four
tub

Name the pictures. Circle the letter that stands for the sound you hear at the end of each picture name.

crib k r (b)	door k (r) b	star k (r) b	bib k r (b)
deer k (r) b	bathtub k r (b)	tiger k (r) b	doorknob k r (b)
hook (k) r b	crab k r (b)	web k r (b)	book (k) r b
mirror k (r) b	guitar k (r) b	beak (k) r b	car k (r) b

17

CONSONANTS: J

The sound at the beginning of **jet** is spelled by the letter **j**.

jet

Name the pictures. Circle each picture whose name begins with the sound of **j**.

judge	jeep	kite	jug
deer	jack-in-the-box	goat	jacks
jacket	juggler	pen	dog
jar	mitten	ball	jewelry

18

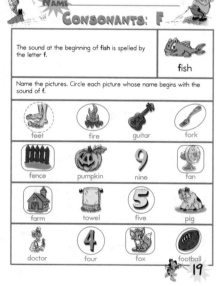

CONSONANTS: F

The sound at the beginning of **fish** is spelled by the letter **f**.

fish

Name the pictures. Circle each picture whose name begins with the sound of **f**.

feet	fire	guitar	fork
fence	pumpkin	nine	fan
farm	towel	five	pig
doctor	four	fox	football

19

CONSONANTS: G

The sound at the beginning of **goat** is spelled by the letter **g**.

goat

Name the pictures. Circle each picture whose name begins with the sound of **g**.

gas	vase	girl	gate
volleyball	guitar	rollerblades	garden
garage	pencil	soap	game
net	golf	goose	needle

20

67

ANSWER KEY

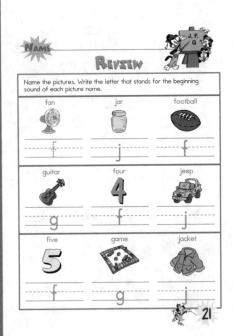

REVIEW

Name the pictures. Write the letter that stands for the beginning sound of each picture name.

fan	jar	football
f	j	f
guitar	four	jeep
g	f	j
five	game	jacket
f	g	j

21

ENDING SOUNDS: F AND G

The sound at the end of **roof** is spelled by the letter f.
The sound at the end of **bag** is spelled by the letter g.

roof
bag

Name the pictures. Circle the letter that stands for the sound you hear at the end of each picture name.

bag	egg	leaf	tag
f / (g)	f / (g)	(f) / g	f / (g)
scarf	pig	flag	frog
(f) / g	f / (g)	f / (g)	f / (g)
wig	rug	log	roof
f / (g)	f / (g)	f / (g)	(f) / g
bug	hoof	leg	dog
f / (g)	(f) / g	f / (g)	f / (g)

22

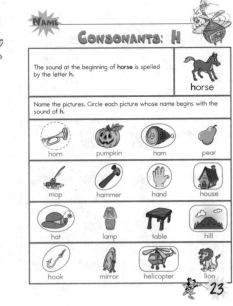

CONSONANTS: H

The sound at the beginning of **horse** is spelled by the letter h.

horse

Name the pictures. Circle each picture whose name begins with the sound of h.

horn	pumpkin	ham	pear
mop	hammer	hand	house
hat	lamp	table	hill
hook	mirror	helicopter	lion

23

CONSONANTS: D

The sound at the beginning of **dog** is spelled by the letter d.

dog

Name the pictures. Circle each picture whose name begins with the sound of d.

duck	bee	doctor	doll
deer	dive	heart	kite
desk	mouse	dishes	belt
feather	door	dominoes	dinosaur

24

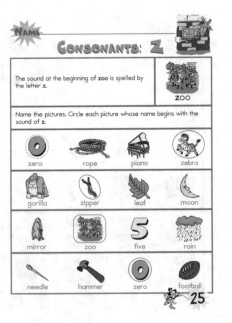

CONSONANTS: Z

The sound at the beginning of **zoo** is spelled by the letter z.

zoo

Name the pictures. Circle each picture whose name begins with the sound of z.

zero	rope	piano	zebra
gorilla	zipper	leaf	moon
mirror	zoo	five	rain
needle	hammer	zero	football

25

REVIEW

Name the pictures. Write the letter that stands for the beginning sound of each picture name.

hammer	deer	hook
h	d	h
zipper	doll	door
z	d	d
hose	zero	dog
h	z	d

26

68

ANSWER KEY

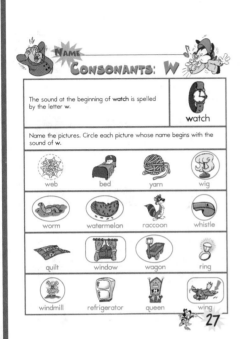

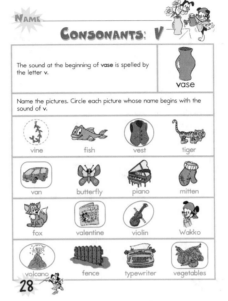

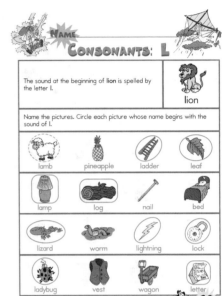

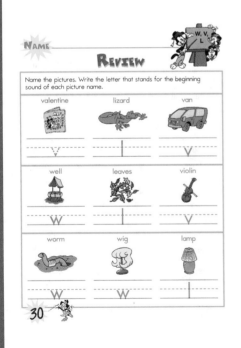

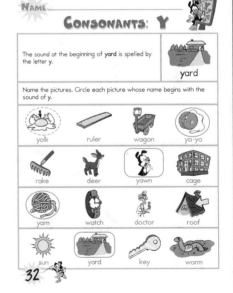

Answer Key

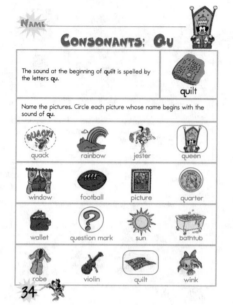

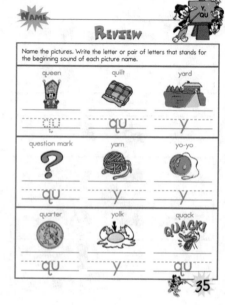

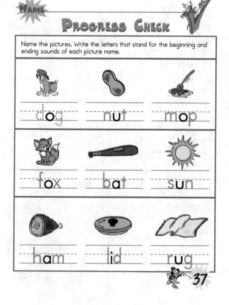

ANSWER KEY

Vowels: Short I

Bib has the short-i sound. This sound is usually spelled by the letter i.

bib

Name the pictures. Circle each picture whose name has the short-i sound.

hill *(circled)*	hat	pig	brick
crib	lemon	bat	dishes
drum	six	milk	tent
quilt	belt	fish	box

39

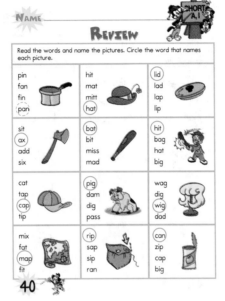

Review

Read the words and name the pictures. Circle the word that names each picture.

pin / fan / fin / **pan** *(circled)*	hit / mat / mitt / **hat** *(circled)*	**lid** *(circled)* / lad / lap / lip
sit / **ax** *(circled)* / add / six	**bat** *(circled)* / bit / miss / mad	**hit** *(circled)* / bag / hat / big
cat / tap / **cap** *(circled)* / tip	**pig** *(circled)* / dam / dig / pass	wag / dig / **wig** *(circled)* / dad
mix / fat / **map** *(circled)* / fit	**rip** *(circled)* / sap / sip / ran	**can** *(circled)* / zip / cap / big

40

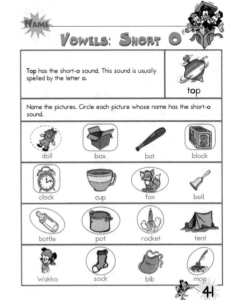

Vowels: Short O

Top has the short-o sound. This sound is usually spelled by the letter o.

top

Name the pictures. Circle each picture whose name has the short-o sound.

doll *(circled)*	box	bat	block
clock	cup	fox	bell
bottle	pot	rocket	tent
Wakko	sock	bib	mop

41

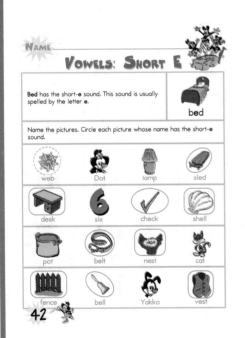

Vowels: Short E

Bed has the short-e sound. This sound is usually spelled by the letter e.

bed

Name the pictures. Circle each picture whose name has the short-e sound.

web *(circled)*	Dot	lamp	sled
desk	six	check	shell
pot	belt	nest	cat
fence	bell	Yakko	vest

42

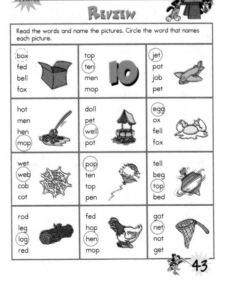

Review

Read the words and name the pictures. Circle the word that names each picture.

box *(circled)* / fed / bell / fox	top / **ten** *(circled)* / men / mop	**jet** *(circled)* / pot / job / pet
hot / men / hen / **mop** *(circled)*	doll / pet / **well** *(circled)* / pot	egg / ox / fell / fox
wet / **web** *(circled)* / cob / cot	**pop** *(circled)* / ten / top / pen	tell / beg / **top** *(circled)* / bed
rod / leg / **log** *(circled)* / red	fed / hop / **hen** *(circled)* / mop	got / **net** *(circled)* / not / get

43

Vowels: Short U

Cup has the short-u sound. This sound is usually spelled by the letter u.

cup

Name the pictures. Circle each picture whose name has the short-u sound.

bun *(circled)*	cot	duck	bus
bed	lips	sun	bat
rug	bib	log	tub
hog	jug	puppy	pigeon

44

ANSWER KEY

REVIEW

Read the words and name the pictures. Circle the word that names each picture.

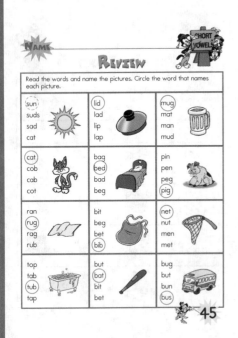

(sun) suds sad cat	lid lad lip lap	mug mat man mud
(cat) cob cab cot	bag (bed) bad beg	pin pen peg (pig)
ran (rug) rag rub	bit beg bet (bib)	(net) nut men met
top tab (tub) tap	but (bat) bit bet	bug but bun (bus)

45

SHORT VOWELS

Name the pictures. Circle the letter that stands for the vowel sound in each picture name. Then write the letter to complete the picture name.

(a) e — bat	i (o) — pot	u (e) — bed
a (u) — sun	(i) a — pig	(o) e — log
(a) o — ax	i (e) — ten	o (u) — bug

46

PROGRESS CHECK

Name the pictures. Write the letter to complete the picture name.

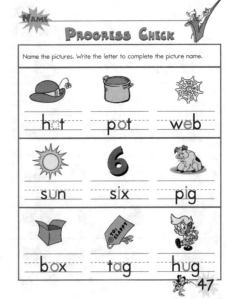

hat	pot	web
sun	six	pig
box	tag	hug

47

VOWELS: LONG A

Rake has the long-a sound. This sound is often spelled by a and silent e.

rake

Name the pictures. Circle each picture whose name has the long-a sound.

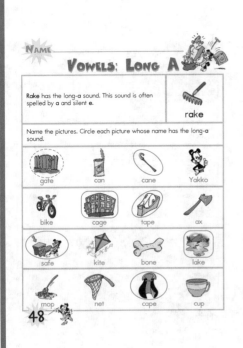

(gate)	can	(cane)	Yakko
bike	(cage)	(tape)	ax
(safe)	kite	bone	(lake)
mop	net	(cape)	cup

48

VOWELS: LONG I

Kite has the long-i sound. This sound is often spelled by i and silent e.

kite

Name the pictures. Circle each picture whose name has the long-i sound.

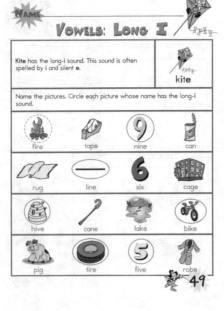

(fire)	tape	(nine)	can
rug	(line)	six	cage
(hive)	cane	lake	(bike)
pig	(tire)	(five)	robe

49

REVIEW

Read the words and name the pictures. Circle the word that names each picture.

time tin tap (tape)	kit can kite (cane)	dim (dime) date dam
pan (van) vine pine	bit (bike) bite big	(ride) rat ran rid
hide (hive) hat hate	miss (mat) mitt man	(dive) dad did date
lad lid like (lake)	sat side (safe) sit	(pine) pal pal pale

50

72

ANSWER KEY

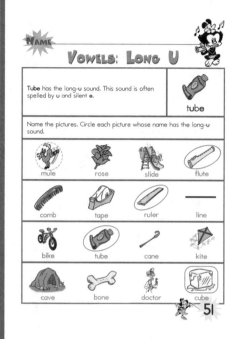

VOWELS: LONG U

Tube has the long-u sound. This sound is often spelled by **u** and silent **e**.

tube

Name the pictures. Circle each picture whose name has the long-**u** sound.

(mule)	rose	slide	flute
comb	tape	ruler	line
bike	(tube)	cane	kite
cave	bone	doctor	(cube)

51

REVIEW

Read the words and name the pictures. Circle the word that names each picture.

cub / cob / cone / (cube)	rode / (ruler) / rod / run	top / toss / tube / (tub)
(mop) / mug / mole / mule	note / (nut) / not / nose	(mule) / mug / moss / mole
rule / (rose) / rod / rug	bone / but / (bus) / box	(top) / tune / tug / tone
rule / run / (rope) / rot	(bone) / box / bus / bun	(note) / nut / nose / not

52

REVIEW

Name the pictures. Write the letters to complete the picture name.

hive	rope	tube
note	mule	cube
bone	vine	lake

53

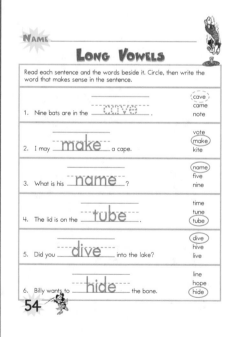

LONG VOWELS

Read each sentence and the words beside it. Circle, then write the word that makes sense in the sentence.

1. Nine bats are in the _____ . — (cave) / came / note
2. I may _____ a cape. — vote / (make) / kite
3. What is his _____ ? — (name) / five / nine
4. The lid is on the _____ . — time / tune / (tube)
5. Did you _____ into the lake? — (dive) / hive / live
6. Billy wants to _____ the bone. — line / hope / (hide)

54

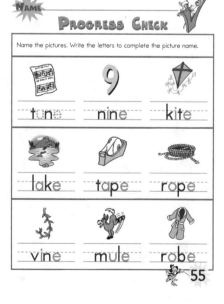

PROGRESS CHECK

Name the pictures. Write the letters to complete the picture name.

tune	nine	kite
lake	tape	rope
vine	mule	robe

55

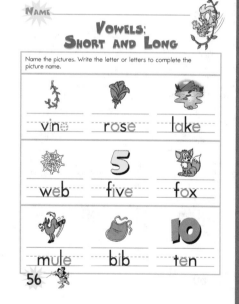

VOWELS: SHORT AND LONG

Name the pictures. Write the letter or letters to complete the picture name.

vine	rose	lake
web	five	fox
mule	bib	ten

56

73

Answer Key

Progress Check

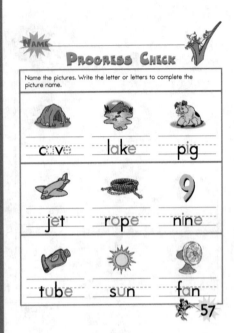

Name

Name the pictures. Write the letter or letters to complete the picture name.

cave · lake · pig
jet · rope · nine
tube · sun · fan

57

S Blends

Name

In some words, the letter s comes before another consonant. To say these words, blend the sound of s with the sound of the consonant that follows it.

stop skate
smile sleep

Name the pictures. In each row, circle the picture or pictures that begin with the same sound as the first picture.

stamp	crib	steps	star
smoke	blender	smile	flag
skate	skunk	broom	skirt
sled	mouse	slide	tree

58

L Blends

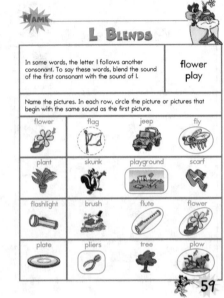

Name

In some words, the letter l follows another consonant. To say these words, blend the sound of the first consonant with the sound of l.

flower
play

Name the pictures. In each row, circle the picture or pictures that begin with the same sound as the first picture.

flower	flag	jeep	fly
plant	skunk	playground	scarf
flashlight	brush	flute	flower
plate	pliers	tree	plow

59

R Blends

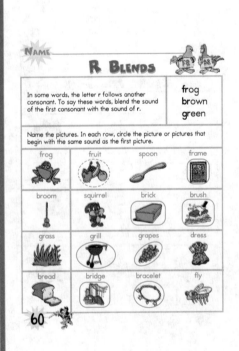

Name

In some words, the letter r follows another consonant. To say these words, blend the sound of the first consonant with the sound of r.

frog
brown
green

Name the pictures. In each row, circle the picture or pictures that begin with the same sound as the first picture.

frog	fruit	spoon	frame
broom	squirrel	brick	brush
grass	grill	grapes	dress
bread	bridge	bracelet	fly

60

Final S Blends

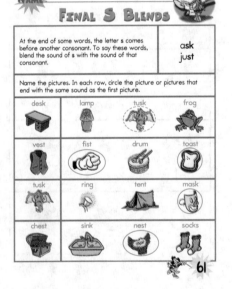

Name

At the end of some words, the letter s comes before another consonant. To say these words, blend the sound of s with the sound of that consonant.

ask
just

Name the pictures. In each row, circle the picture or pictures that end with the same sound as the first picture.

desk	lamp	tusk	frog
vest	fist	drum	toast
tusk	ring	tent	mask
chest	sink	nest	socks

61

Progress Check

Name

Read the words below. Then name the pictures. Write the word that names the picture.

| drum | sled | desk | flag | snake |
| crab | nest | plate | frog | |

crab · flag · snake
sled · frog · desk
drum · plate · nest

62

74

ANSWER KEY

Look for all of these entertaining and educational titles in

The McGraw-Hill Junior Academic™ Workbook Series

Toddler

My Colors Go 'Round	ISBN 1-57768-208-4	UPC 6-09746-45118-5
My 1, 2, 3's	ISBN 1-57768-218-1	UPC 6-09746-45128-4
My A, B, C's	ISBN 1-57768-228-9	UPC 6-09746-45138-3
My Ups and Downs	ISBN 1-57768-238-6	UPC 6-09746-45148-2

Preschool

MATH	ISBN 1-57768-209-2	UPC 6-09746-45119-2
READING	ISBN 1-57768-219-X	UPC 6-09746-45129-1
VOWEL SOUNDS	ISBN 1-57768-229-7	UPC 6-09746-45139-0
SOUND PATTERNS	ISBN 1-57768-239-4	UPC 6-09746-45149-9

Kindergarten

MATH	ISBN 1-57768-200-9	UPC 6-09746-45110-9
READING	ISBN 1-57768-210-6	UPC 6-09746-45120-8
PHONICS	ISBN 1-57768-220-3	UPC 6-09746-45130-7
THINKING SKILLS	ISBN 1-57768-230-0	UPC 6-09746-45140-6

Grade 1

MATH	ISBN 1-57768-201-7	UPC 6-09746-45111-6
READING	ISBN 1-57768-211-4	UPC 6-09746-45121-5
PHONICS	ISBN 1-57768-221-1	UPC 6-09746-45131-4
WORD BUILDERS	ISBN 1-57768-231-9	UPC 6-09746-45141-3

Grade 2

MATH	ISBN 1-57768-202-5	UPC 6-09746-45112-3
READING	ISBN 1-57768-212-2	UPC 6-09746-45122-2
PHONICS	ISBN 1-57768-222-X	UPC 6-09746-45132-1
WORD BUILDERS	ISBN 1-57768-232-7	UPC 6-09746-45142-0

It's Serious Fun!!

Software titles available from
McGRAW-HILL HOME INTERACTIVE

The skills taught in school are now available at home! These titles are
now available in retail stores and teacher supply stores everywhere.
All titles meet school guidelines and are based on
The McGraw-Hill Companies classroom software titles.

MATH GRADES 1 & 2

These math programs are a great way to teach and reinforce skills used in everyday situations. Fun, friendly characters need help with their math skills. Everyone's friend, Nubby the stubby pencil, will help kids master the math in the Numbers Quiz show. Foggy McHammer, a carpenter, needs some help building his playhouse so that all the boards will fit together! Julio Bambino's kitchen antics will surely burn his pastries if you don't help him set the clock timer correctly! We can't forget Turbo Tomato, a fruit with a passion for adventure, who needs help calculating his daredevil stunts.

Math Grades 1 & 2 use a tested, proven approach to reinforcing your child's math skills while keeping him or her intrigued with Nubby and his collection of crazy friends.

TITLE	ISBN	PRICE
Grade 1: Nubby's Quiz Show	1-57768-011-1	$14.95
Grade 2: Foggy McHammer's Treehouse	1-57768-012-X	$14.95

MISSION MASTERS™ MATH AND LANGUAGE ARTS

The Mission Masters™—Pauline, Rakeem, Mia, and T.J.—need your help. The Mission Masters™ are a team of young agents working for the Intelliforce Agency, a high-level cooperative whose goal is to maintain order on our rather unruly planet. From within the agency's top secret Command Control Center, the agency's central computer, M5, has detected a threat...and guess what—you're the agent assigned to the mission!

MISSION MASTERS™ MATH GRADES 3, 4 & 5

This series of exciting activities encourages young mathematicians to challenge themselves and their math skills to overcome the perils of villains and other planetary threats. Skills reinforced include: analyzing and solving real-world problems, estimation, measurements, geometry, whole numbers, fractions, graphs, and patterns.

TITLE	ISBN	PRICE
Grade 3: Mission Masters™ Defeat Dirty D!	1-57768-013-8	$19.95
Grade 4: Mission Masters™ Alien Encounter	1-57768-014-6	$19.95
Grade 5: Mission Masters™ Meet Mudflat Moe	1-57768-015-4	$19.95

MISSION MASTERS™ LANGUAGE ARTS GRADES 3, 4 & 5

This series invites children to apply their language skills to defeat unscrupulous characters and to overcome other earthly dangers. Skills reinforced include: language mechanics and usage, punctuation, spelling, vocabulary, reading comprehension, and creative writing.

TITLE	ISBN	PRICE
Grade 3: Mission Masters™ Freezing Frenzy	1-57768-023-5	$24.95
Grade 4: Mission Masters™ Network Nightmare	1-57768-024-3	$24.95
Grade 5: Mission Masters™ Mummy Mysteries	1-57768-025-1	$24.95

Look for these and other exciting software titles at a retail store near you.
All titles for Windows 3.1™, Windows '95™, and Macintosh™.
Visit us on the Internet at
www.MHkids.com

Offers a selection of workbooks to meet all your needs.

Look for all of these fine educational workbooks
in the McGraw-Hill Learning Materials SPECTRUM Series.
All workbooks meet school curriculum guidelines and correspond to
The McGraw-Hill Companies classroom textbooks.

SPECTRUM SERIES

GEOGRAPHY

Full-color, three-part lessons strengthen geography knowledge and map reading skills. Focusing on five geographic themes including location, place, human/environmental interaction, movement, and regions. Over 150 pages. Glossary of geographical terms and answer key included.

TITLE	ISBN	PRICE
Grade 3, Communities	1-57768-153-3	$7.95
Grade 4, Regions	1-57768-154-1	$7.95
Grade 5, USA	1-57768-155-X	$7.95
Grade 6, World	1-57768-156-8	$7.95

MATH

Features easy-to-follow instructions that give students a clear path to success. This series has comprehensive coverage of the basic skills, helping children to master math fundamentals. Over 150 pages. Answer key included.

TITLE	ISBN	PRICE
Grade 1	1-57768-111-8	$6.95
Grade 2	1-57768-112-6	$6.95
Grade 3	1-57768-113-4	$6.95
Grade 4	1-57768-114-2	$6.95
Grade 5	1-57768-115-0	$6.95
Grade 6	1-57768-116-9	$6.95
Grade 7	1-57768-117-7	$6.95
Grade 8	1-57768-118-5	$6.95

PHONICS

Provides everything children need to build multiple skills in language. Focusing on phonics, structural analysis, and dictionary skills, this series also offers creative ideas for using phonics and word study skills in other language arts. Over 200 pages. Answer key included.

TITLE	ISBN	PRICE
Grade K	1-57768-120-7	$6.95
Grade 1	1-57768-121-5	$6.95
Grade 2	1-57768-122-3	$6.95
Grade 3	1-57768-123-1	$6.95
Grade 4	1-57768-124-X	$6.95
Grade 5	1-57768-125-8	$6.95
Grade 6	1-57768-126-6	$6.95

READING

This full-color series creates an enjoyable reading environment, even for below-average readers. Each book contains captivating content, colorful characters, and compelling illustrations, so children are eager to find out what happens next. Over 150 pages. Answer key included.

TITLE	ISBN	PRICE
Grade K	1-57768-130-4	$6.95
Grade 1	1-57768-131-2	$6.95
Grade 2	1-57768-132-0	$6.95
Grade 3	1-57768-133-9	$6.95
Grade 4	1-57768-134-7	$6.95
Grade 5	1-57768-135-5	$6.95
Grade 6	1-57768-136-3	$6.95

SPELLING

This full-color series links spelling to reading and writing and increases skills in words and meanings, consonant and vowel spellings, and proofreading practice. Over 200 pages. Speller dictionary and answer key included.

TITLE	ISBN	PRICE
Grade 1	1-57768-161-4	$7.95
Grade 2	1-57768-162-2	$7.95
Grade 3	1-57768-163-0	$7.95
Grade 4	1-57768-164-9	$7.95
Grade 5	1-57768-165-7	$7.95
Grade 6	1-57768-166-5	$7.95

WRITING

Lessons focus on creative and expository writing using clearly stated objectives and pre-writing exercises. Eight essential reading skills are applied. Activities include main idea, sequence, comparison, detail, fact and opinion, cause and effect, and making a point. Over 130 pages. Answer key included.

TITLE	ISBN	PRICE
Grade 1	1-57768-141-X	$6.95
Grade 2	1-57768-142-8	$6.95
Grade 3	1-57768-143-6	$6.95
Grade 4	1-57768-144-4	$6.95
Grade 5	1-57768-145-2	$6.95
Grade 6	1-57768-146-0	$6.95
Grade 7	1-57768-147-9	$6.95
Grade 8	1-57768-148-7	$6.95

TEST PREP from the Nation's #1 Testing Company

Prepares children to do their best on current editions of the five major standardized tests. Activities reinforce test-taking skills through examples, tips, practice, and timed exercises. Subjects include reading, math, and language. Over 150 pages. Answer key included.

TITLE	ISBN	PRICE
Grade 3	1-57768-103-7	$8.95
Grade 4	1-57768-104-5	$8.95
Grade 5	1-57768-105-3	$8.95
Grade 6	1-57768-106-1	$8.95
Grade 7	1-57768-107-X	$8.95
Grade 8	1-57768-108-8	$8.95